Louis Pasteur

Liz Miles

www.heinemann.co.uk/library

Visit our website to find out more information about **Heinemann** books.

To order:

☎ Phone 44 (0) 1865 888112

📄 Send a fax to 44 (0) 1865 314091

💻 Visit the Heinemann Bookshop at **www.heinemann.co.uk/library** to browse our catalogue and order online.

Heinemann Library is an imprint of **Pearson Education Limited**, a company incorporated in England and Wales having its registered office at Edinburgh Gate, Harlow, Essex, CM20 2JE – Registered company number: 00872828 Heinemann is a registered trademark of Pearson Education Limited.

Text © Pearson Education Limited 2009
First published in hardback in 2009
The moral rights of the proprietor have been asserted.

Edited by Louise Galpine and Catherine Clarke
Designed by Kimberly R. Miracle and Betsy Wernert
Original illustrations © Pearson Education Limited 2008, Illustrated by Mapping Specialists
Picture research by Mica Brancic
Originated by Modern Age
Printed in China by Leo Paper Group

ISBN 978- 0-43-104484-2 (hardback)
12 11 10 09 08
10 9 8 7 6 5 4 3 2 1

British Library Cataloguing in Publication Data
Miles, Liz
Louis Pasteur. - (Levelled biographies)
540.9'2
A full catalogue record for this book is available from the British Library.

Acknowledgments
The publishers would like to thank the following for permission to reproduce photographs: © Alamy p. **25** (Holt Studios International Ltd); © Corbis pp. **5** (The Gallery Collection), **14** (Bettmann), **16** (Etsa/ Peter Carlsson), (Visuals Unlimited), **21** (B. Borrell Casals; Frank Lane Picture Agency), **22** (Charles O'Rear), **23** (Sandro Vannini), **31** (Bettmann), **41** (Andreas Lander/dpa); © Getty Images p. **24** (After Franz Xavier Winterhalter), **40** (Edward Gooch); © Mary Evans Picture Library p. **11**; © Popperfoto p. **39**; © Rex Features p. **9** (Roger-Viollet); © Science Museum p. **29**; © Science Photo Library pp. **4**, **10**, **12** (Sinclair Stammers), **18** (Andrew Syred), **19** (Jean-Loup Charmet); © The Art Archive p. **33** (Marc Charmet); © The Bridgeman Art Library pp. **8** (Musée Pasteur, Institut Pasteur, Paris, France, Archives Charmet), **35** (Archives Charmet/Académie Nationale de Médecine, Paris, France), **37** (Archives Charmet/ Académie Nationale de Médecine, Paris, France); © The Pasteur Institute pp. **15**, **27**; © Wellcome Images p. **7**.

Cover photograph of a portrait of Louis Pasteur reproduced with permission of © Corbis (Archivo Iconografico, S.A.).

We would like to thank Nancy Harris for her invaluable help in the preparation of this book.

CONTENTS

Some words are shown in bold, **like this**. You can find out what they mean by looking in the glossary.

Hard Times

In 1822, Louis Pasteur was born into a world that was very different from ours. Terrible illnesses such as **typhoid fever** and **cholera** spread fast, killing millions of people. When Louis was 10 years old, cholera arrived in France, the country where he lived. Thousands of townspeople died after suffering from **symptoms** such as fever and vomiting.

Dirty conditions

Few medicines existed and no one understood why people caught diseases from each other. The importance of **hygiene** in controlling the spread of **germs** was not known. People did not wash their hands or keep their homes clean. Even hospitals were dangerous places to go because the wards were dirty.

During Louis' childhood, sheets or clothes from cholera victims were washed in rivers. The dirty river water full of cholera germs was then used for drinking water.

Tiny but deadly

When Louis Pasteur was born, scientists were working hard to stop the spread of diseases. They used **microscopes** to examine the tiny world of germs. But they did not really understand what they were looking at.

Pasteur's amazing research and discoveries brought about the control of many of these tiny, deadly creatures. His work was to save countless lives. Pasteur became known as one of the "fathers" of modern medicine.

A country in trouble

During Pasteur's lifetime, he saw **revolutions** and unrest in France. Three kings and one **emperor** gained and lost their crowns while Louis was alive. **Governments** in France rose and fell, too.

Pasteur spent much of his life looking at germs in his laboratory.

SCHOOL DAYS

Louis Pasteur was born in Dole, France. He was born on 27 December 1822.

Family background

Louis' mother, Jeanne, was the daughter of a gardener. His father, Jean-Joseph, had served as a soldier. He fought for France and its **emperor**, Napoleon Bonaparte, and was given a medal for his services.

By the time Louis was born, his father had returned to his job as a **tanner**. The family lived above his father's workshop, the tannery.

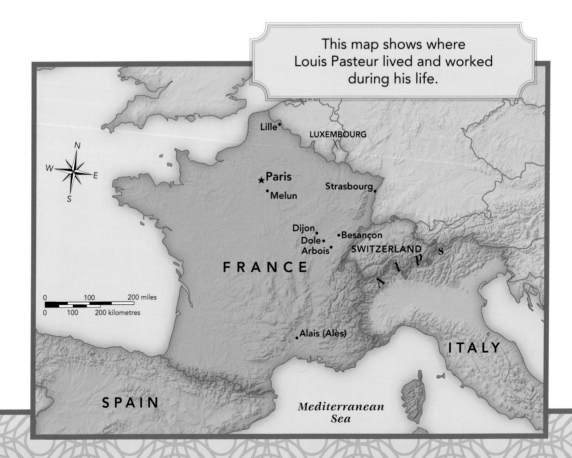

This map shows where Louis Pasteur lived and worked during his life.

This is a photograph of Dole, the small town where Louis was born.

On the move

Early in 1827, when Louis was four years old, the family moved to another French town, called Arbois. A river ran next to their new home, where Louis loved to play and fish with his friends. Louis enjoyed his childhood, except for one thing – his schoolwork.

A father's hope

Louis' father wanted his son to train to be a teacher. But during his first school years, Louis did not seem to be clever enough. He worked slowly and his test results were poor. There was no sign that Louis would be a teacher, let alone a famous scientist!

A tanner's life

Tanners made leather. It was a dirty, smelly process. First, the flesh was scraped off the fresh hides (skins) of cows and sheep. Next, the hides were soaked in mixtures of dog, pigeon, or chicken **excrement** to soften them. The hides were then placed in pits in the ground, with oak bark and water. After a year, the hides finally turned into leather.

Artistic skills

At 13 years old, Louis had just one talent – he was brilliant at art. He thought of becoming a full-time artist but one of his teachers told him that he was a clever thinker and should go on with his schooling. So, although many children left school to earn money, Louis continued with his studies.

Louis painted this picture of his mother when he was just 13 years old.

Homesick

In 1838, aged 15, Louis was sent to a school in Paris, the capital of France. His father hoped that Louis would then go on to the École Normale Supérieure in Paris. This was a famous college where students were trained to be university teachers and professors. But after just six weeks in the busy city, Louis was too homesick to stay. His father brought him home.

When Louis was in Paris, missing his home and family terribly, he said to a friend:

"If I could only smell the odour of the tannery, I am sure I would feel better."

Back on track

Back at his old school in Arbois, Louis started to paint again, but he did not give up his dream of going to the École Normale. In 1839, 17-year-old Louis moved to the Royal College in nearby Besançon and began to prepare for the École's entrance exam.

It was Louis' goal to go to the École Normale Supérieure in Paris.

EXCITED BY SCIENCE

At the Royal College in Besançon, Louis studied hard. In the summer of 1842, he passed his exams. Now he had an even more important challenge – the entrance exam for the École Normale.

Not good enough

Louis passed the first part of the exam but then he surprised everyone – he refused to take the second part! In the first exam he had come 15th out of 22 students. The result was not good enough for 19-year-old Louis, he wanted to do better.

This drawing shows Louis when he was a student in Paris.

Louis rarely explored the busy city of Paris. He preferred to stay indoors and study **physics** or **chemistry**.

Studying and teaching

Louis decided to study science for another year, this time in Paris. By October 1842, he was living in Paris and too busy to be homesick. To earn money to pay for his lodgings, he taught younger students mathematics. Afterwards, he went to classes. He often joined the crowds at talks by Jean-Baptiste Dumas, a famous **chemist**. Louis was inspired by Dumas' love of science.

Paris
Paris was busy, noisy, and expensive. Few people could afford all that a student needed such as the college courses, paper, books, pens, and ink. Food, lodging, candles, and wood for the fire had to be paid for, too.

Just rewards

In August 1843, Louis passed the exam to go to the École Normale to study science. This time, 4th from the top of his class, he was proud of his result.

Hard work

Louis worked hard, often for 12 hours a day, at the École Normale. In 1846, he passed the final exam needed to become a professor. He was offered a teaching job as professor of **physics** (study of matter and energy). But by now he wanted to work in a **laboratory** and study substances.

What next?

A famous **chemist** called Balard took Louis on as an assistant. In Balard's laboratory, Louis could do research of his own. He chose to study the world of **crystals**. Lots of substances, such as ice, salt, and diamonds, are made of the tiny, solid objects we call crystals.

Louis used a special light to show the differences between crystals. This photograph shows tarctic crystals lit by the same kind of light. The crystals bend the light.

Spot the difference

Louis wanted to solve a problem that scientists had been struggling with. What was the difference between two identical-looking types of crystal, called **tartrate acid** and **paratartrate acid**? When Louis shone a special light on these crystals, the light behaved differently. But the crystals looked the same.

In 1847, after a lot of research, Louis found the answer. The paratartrate acid had a slightly different structure. It was made up of two types of crystal, not one. The two types were very similar. The only difference was that they were a mirror image of each other.

This diagram shows the two types of crystal in paratartrate acid – the shaded parts show how they are a mirror image of each other.

Success!

Although it does not seem very exciting to us, Louis' discovery was very important. It provided a greater understanding of the structure of crystals. At the age of 26, Louis had become noticed in the world of important scientists.

Louis later recalled his discovery:

"I remember hurrying from the laboratory ... so happy that I was shaking all over."

The National Guard helped to stop the riots in Paris in 1848.

Change of government

In February 1848, **riots** broke out on the streets of Paris. A **revolution** followed, forcing the unpopular king, Louis-Philippe, to leave the country. A new **government** was formed.

Louis' parents heard reports of shootings, and tried to persuade him to leave Paris. Unwilling to leave his work, instead he did his bit to try to stop the riots. In April, he joined the National Guard, a peacekeeping army.

A tragic death

In May, Louis' mother became very ill. Louis rushed home, but his mother had already died. He felt guilty, thinking that she had become ill from worry over his safety in Paris.

Family or work?

Louis' father now had three unmarried daughters to look after. In those days, few women left home until they married. Louis felt he should help to support them. In September, he got a job as a school teacher in Dijon, not far from his father's home. But Louis really wanted to continue his research. In January 1849, he left to become a professor of **chemistry** at the University of Strasbourg.

A speedy romance

Less than a month later, Louis met 22-year-old Marie Laurent, a **rector's** daughter. He soon asked her to marry him. Their wedding day was 29 May 1849. Marie accepted that her husband would always put his work first. Years later, she had to write to their son to explain that Louis was too busy to send a letter: "He cannot take a moment away from his work," she explained.

This is a painting of Louis' wife, Marie, around 1850.

STRANGE LITTLE "CREATURES"

Louis Pasteur spent five, mostly happy, years at the University of Strasbourg, studying **crystals** and teaching. In 1850, the first of his four daughters was born. In 1851, his only son, Jean-Baptiste, was born.

Moving on

By 1854, Pasteur's work on crystals had come to an end. The family moved to Lille in northern France, where Pasteur took the job of **chemistry** professor at the University's new science department.

Sticky and sour

Monsieur Bigo, a businessman, asked Pasteur to help him solve a problem. Bigo had a factory where beet juice was made into alcohol. Beets are root vegetables. The process of **fermentation** was used in the factory. The alcohol was sold to make medicines. But some of the fermenting beet juice was turning sticky and sour, and had to be thrown away.

Beetroot is a type of beet. Pasteur studied fermentation to help stop beet juice going sour.

Living yeast

Pasteur set about studying fermentation. Scientists knew that **yeast** was probably involved in fermentation because they had seen yeast in fermenting liquids. But they did not agree on why the yeast was there. Pasteur focused his **microscope** on the yeast in a sample of fermented beet juice.

Pasteur was amazed at what he saw. The yeast was alive! It was feeding on the sugars in the beet juice. As it fed, it grew little buds that broke off and multiplied. As it ate the sugars, it broke them down and gave off alcohol. It also gave off a **gas** called carbon dioxide.

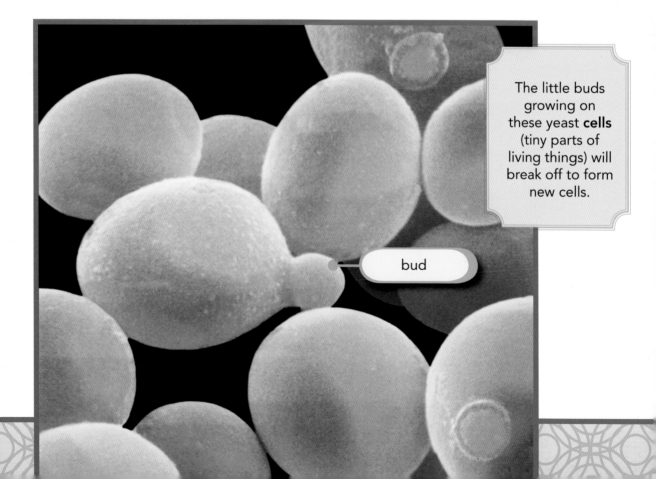

bud

The little buds growing on these yeast **cells** (tiny parts of living things) will break off to form new cells.

Dancing rods

Now that Pasteur understood the workings of **yeast**, he was able to solve the mystery of Bigo's sour beet juice. Pasteur examined a drop of the sour mixture through his **microscope**. There was no yeast there.

Pasteur then noticed some sticky specks. The microscope showed that just one speck was made up of millions of moving creatures. They were rod-shaped and kept multiplying. Later, he called them **microbes**.

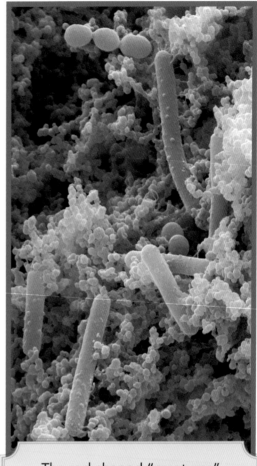

The rod-shaped "creatures" Louis saw were **bacteria**. They are also found in yoghurt.

Yeast "soup"

Pasteur experimented. He put some of the rod-shaped microbes into a boiled mixture of water, sugar, and yeast. He watched to see if it turned sour. It did. Pasteur realized that the microbes had somehow destroyed the yeast. They had also turned the sugar into an **acid**. It was the acid that had turned Bigo's beet juice sour.

The problem is solved

Pasteur concluded that there were two types of **fermentation**. One involved yeast, and the other involved the rod-shaped microbes. He did not know where the rod-shaped microbes came from. Bigo was shown how to use a microscope to check his beet juice for them regularly. Pasteur explained that if a single microbe was spotted, the whole mixture should be thrown away. The container should then be cleaned thoroughly.

Microbiology

From then on, microbes were studied to see how they could be useful or deadly. The study of microbes became a new science, called microbiology. This new science led to an understanding of many human illnesses.

Winemakers use fermentation, so Pasteur's discoveries helped the wine industry, too.

Germs in the air

In October 1857, Pasteur went to work at his old college, the École Normale in Paris. He set up his own **laboratory** in the attic of the college.

Pasteur's mission

Pasteur had a mission – he wanted to prove his theory that **microbes** came from the air. He believed they could reproduce themselves (multiply). This view challenged a popular belief at the time, called spontaneous generation (see box).

Finding the evidence

To prove that microbes were carried in the air, Pasteur invented a pump to bring air from the street into his laboratory. He passed the air through a cotton **filter** to take out the dust. Next, he examined the dust. As he thought, there were lots of microbes in it. They were the same kind as those he had seen in rotting matter, like meat. He later thought that wherever such microbes landed, they could be dangerous and even cause diseases.

Believers in spontaneous generation still weren't convinced. Balard, now an elderly professor of **chemistry**, made a suggestion. He thought Pasteur should use some strange new flasks, with swan-shaped necks, in his next experiments.

Believers in spontaneous generation once thought that even the maggots in rotten meat came from nowhere. Then, in 1668, a scientist proved that flies had laid eggs on the meat, and the maggots had hatched from the eggs.

Spontaneous generation

Spontaneous generation was the belief that living things, like microbes, could appear out of nowhere. At one time it was thought that a mouse could just grow out of a sack of grain!

Tragic loss

In September 1859, Pasteur's eldest daughter, nine-year-old Jeanne, died suddenly of **typhoid fever**. Pasteur had begun to suspect that **microbes** caused diseases like typhoid. He began to research his ideas.

Success!

Pasteur used Balard's swan-necked flasks to prove that microbes do not appear from nowhere. He filled the flasks with a **yeast** mixture. He boiled it to kill any microbes, and then left the flasks unsealed. Air passed down the swan-shaped necks to the mixture. But any microbe-carrying dust in the air was blocked at the U-bend in the necks. Microbes did not reach the mixture. Even after several days, no microbes appeared in the mixture. This showed that microbes don't appear from nowhere. Pasteur then tipped some of the flasks. This made the dust in the U-bend fall down into the mixture. Very soon, microbes appeared in the mixture. This showed that the microbes came from dust.

Swan-shaped neck

U-bend

This is one of Pasteur's swan-necked flasks. Even today, a century later, his dust-free flasks are still clear of microbes.

Mountaineering

In 1860, Pasteur gathered air from different locations. This is what he found:

Location	Number of flasks filled with air	Number of the flasks found to contain microbes
Mont Blanc (high mountain in the Alps)	20	1
Hillside near Arbois	20	8
Yard in Paris	10	10
Cellar	10	1

Mont Blanc in the Alps was one of the places where Pasteur collected air. He discovered that this air was very clean.

He found fewer microbes in the clean mountain air and the still air of a cellar. Pasteur had discovered that there were different amounts of microbes in different places.

Napoleon III, emperor of France, asked Louis to help the winemakers.

Help for the winemakers

News of Louis' experiments spread across France. Napoleon III, **emperor** of France, heard about them, too. In 1863, he asked Louis to help France's winemakers.

Wine is made from **fermented** grapes, but something was going wrong. The wine was turning cloudy and bitter. In 1864, Louis set up a **laboratory** in Arbois to study the problem. He bought a vineyard, too, so that he could study how grapes are grown.

Killing microbes

Louis examined some bitter wine, and spotted **microbes**. Louis wondered how the microbes could be destroyed. He knew that boiling a mixture killed any microbes, but boiling wine made it taste bad. Finally, he worked out that if wine was heated at a temperature below boiling for a few moments, the microbes were killed. But the flavour of the wine was unchanged.

Pasteurization

The method, known as "Pasteur's process", became widely used. It was used to preserve not only wine but many other drinks and foods, too. We now benefit from **pasteurization** every day. It means that the milk we drink is free from dangerous **bacteria**. It also means that milk and other foods keep longer without going bad.

"Germs are everywhere"

In April 1864, Louis decided that the whole world must be warned that microbes, or germs, get everywhere. During a talk to writers, scientists, and government leaders, he shone a beam of light over their heads. He pointed to the dust and told them that there were lots of germs there.

Modern machinery is now used for pasteurizing milk.

SILK AND SADNESS

In 1865, the silk industry faced a crisis. They turned to Louis. The silk-makers' problem was that a disease called pébrine was killing the silkworms. When **chemist** J. B. Dumas asked Louis to help them, Louis was still busy with **pasteurization**. But Louis knew that the silk industry was important to France, so he agreed.

Silk

Silk is a lightweight, expensive cloth made of threads from silkworms. Silkworms are a type of caterpillar. The silkworms make and spin the thread to form a cocoon, or **chrysalis**, around themselves. Silk-makers unwind the thread from the cocoons, and then weave it into silk.

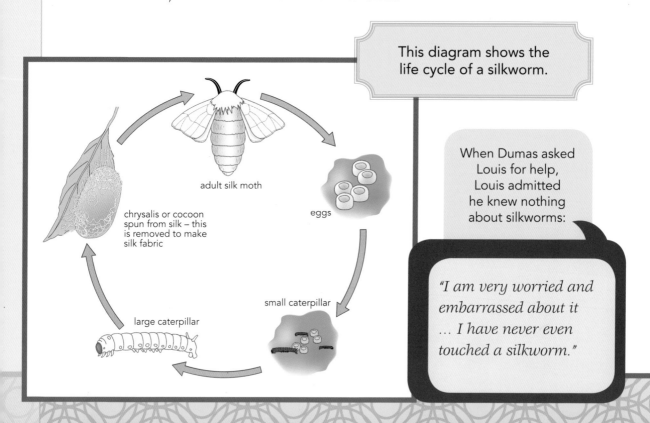

This diagram shows the life cycle of a silkworm.

adult silk moth

eggs

chrysalis or cocoon spun from silk – this is removed to make silk fabric

large caterpillar

small caterpillar

When Dumas asked Louis for help, Louis admitted he knew nothing about silkworms:

"I am very worried and embarrassed about it … I have never even touched a silkworm."

Failure first

Alais was a silkworm-farm region in southern France. Louis travelled from Paris to Alais every summer for three years before he found success. He first suggested that they keep any diseased worms away from healthy worms, so the healthy worms were not infected. But the healthy worms still caught the disease.

Personal tragedies

In June 1865, Louis heard that his father was very ill. By the time he got home, his father had died. More tragedies followed. In September, Louis' youngest daughter, 2-year-old Camille, died from a liver illness. In May 1866, 12-year-old daughter Cécile died of **typhoid fever**. After each terrible loss, Pasteur tried to get over his sadness by losing himself in his work.

After Cécile's death, only two of Marie and Louis' five children still survived. This photograph shows Jean-Baptiste, Cécile, and Marie-Louise.

Not one, but two

Louis struggled on to find an answer to the silkworm problem. He could not understand why the moths from healthy silkworms laid diseased eggs. Louis and his assistants examined silkworms and eggs through **microscopes**. At last, a discovery! There were two diseases attacking the silkworms, not one. The newly discovered disease (called flacherie) was caused by a **microbe**. Moths, eggs, and worms carried the microbe around.

Valuable advice

Louis realised that the flacherie microbes came to life in hot conditions. He told the silkworm farmers to keep the worms in cool rooms. He explained that diseased worms in clean, dry rooms would also live longer than those in dirty, damp places. He showed the farmers how to use a microscope. If they saw any living microbes in worms, the worms should be removed and destroyed.

A hero

In 1868, when Louis went for his visit to the silk farms, he found that most of the worms were well. The silk-makers had silk again, and the clothes industry was saved. Louis returned to Paris as a hero.

This drawing shows all the stages of the silk-making process. At the top of the drawing you can see farmers storing their worms on shelves in a clean, airy room.

Paralysed

Since 1865, Louis had spent the summers in Alais. For the rest of each year he was in Paris, busily teaching, writing papers, and researching. Then, all his work came to a stop on the night of 19 October 1868. Louis had a **stroke**. It left him paralysed, unable to talk or walk. His family, friends, and supporters rushed to his bedside.

FIND THE GERM!

Slowly, Louis recovered. He began to talk again and was able to move. Within three months he was giving advice to silkworm farmers from his bed. Soon, Louis could walk again.

Human suffering

After losing two of his children to **typhoid fever**, Louis knew about the horrors of human disease. When the **Franco-Prussian war** began in 1870, Louis' only son, Jean-Baptiste, joined the army. Louis was so worried about his son that in January 1871 he went to look for him near the Swiss border.

Louis was relieved to find Jean-Baptiste. But he was horrified to see so many injured, diseased, and dying soldiers. Later, it was found that of the 13,000 wounded soldiers who had surgery during the war (1870–71), 10,000 died of **infections**. Louis was eager to join the battle against infection.

Joseph Lister

In fact, Louis had already helped in the battle. His work on **microbes** and **proof** that dangerous microbes are in the air had inspired an English doctor called Joseph Lister. In 1865, Lister had invented an **antiseptic**. It was called carbolic **acid**. It successfully kept patients' wounds free of infection from airborne microbes.

By the 1870s, many surgeons used Lister's carbolic acid in hospitals. The antiseptic meant that far fewer people died of infectious diseases after surgery. In one hospital, instead of 60 percent of patients dying of infections, only 4 per cent died.

Lister's carbolic spray was used to **sterilize** operating theatres. This painting shows Lister using the spray during an operation, around 1865.

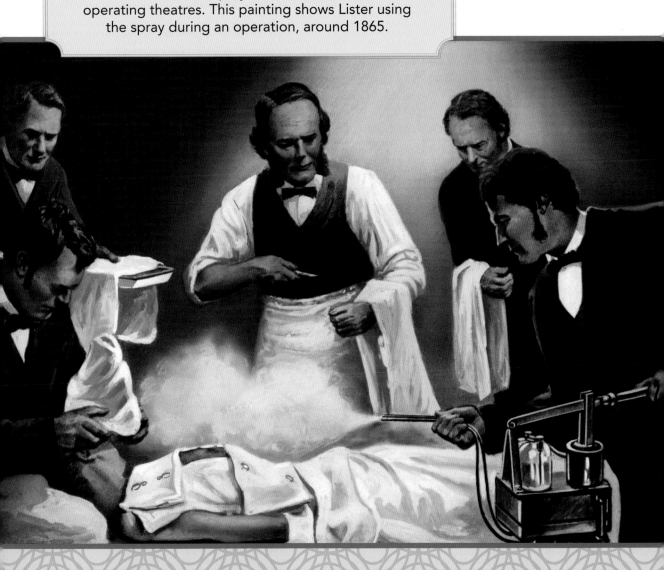

Cotton wool dressings

Around this time, French doctor Alphonse Guérin invited Louis to see how he, too, had learned from Louis' work. He was using cotton wool dressings to stop microbes from infecting wounds.

It was Louis' first visit to a hospital and he saw that Guérin's dressings were a good barrier against any germs. But he also noted that doctors had dirty hands and the wards were unclean. He suggested:

- dressings should be **sterilized** (cleaned thoroughly) by heating
- wounds should be cleaned before they are dressed
- surgeon's hands and instruments should be sterilized
- water for washing wounds should be boiled first
- hospital wards should be kept clean and well-aired.

All this may seem like common sense to us. But in those days, no one had thought of such things before.

Stopping disease

By 1877, Louis was inspired to focus on finding germs that caused diseases. Louis' idea was that one microbe, or germ, could cause one disease. He believed that it was possible to find and isolate the germ. Then, the germ could be killed or controlled to stop the disease spreading.

Past attempt

Back in 1865, hundreds of people in Paris died from **cholera** each day. Louis and other scientists tried to help by finding the cholera germ. Louis looked for the germ in air pumped up from a cholera ward, but found nothing. If he had looked in the blood of a patient, he would have found it.

This engraving shows Empress Eugenie (Napoleon's wife) visiting patients sick from cholera, in 1865.

CHICKENS, SHEEP, AND COWS

By 1877, Louis had a large new **laboratory** in Paris. The French **government** had spent several years building it for him.

In 1879, a disease called chicken **cholera** had killed a tenth of all the chickens in France. Louis soon found the **microbe** that caused it. He grew more of the microbes in chicken broth to use in experiments.

A lucky mistake

In 1880, Louis spent the summer in Arbois. It is said that his assistants forgot the **cultures** (bacteria they had grown) and allowed them to dry out by mistake. On his return, Louis injected the microbes from the dried cultures into some chickens. They did not get the disease. Then he injected fresh, multiplying cholera microbes into the same chickens. Still, they did not get the disease.

Vaccines from old broth

Louis realised that the dried out cultures had worked as a **vaccine**. A vaccine is a weaker form of a disease. It makes the body of a person or animal more able to fight off a stronger form of the disease later. The weaker form of cholera made the chickens' bodies able to fight off the more powerful form.

Edward Jenner and cowpox

Louis had remembered the work of the English doctor, Edward Jenner. Jenner made the first human vaccination. He injected a person with a weak form of cowpox disease. The person's body was then able to fight off a dangerous disease called smallpox.

Jenner's first smallpox **vaccination** was given to a boy in 1796. Soon people were being vaccinated all over the world and smallpox was wiped out.

Deadly anthrax

In the 1800s, the disease **anthrax** was sweeping through France, killing thousands of cows and sheep. In each animal, the multiplying **bacteria** created blistering boils on the skin. It also poisoned the blood.

Robert Koch

In 1873, a German scientist, Robert Koch, had spotted multiplying microbes in the blood of animals that had died from anthrax. It was not in the blood of healthy animals. Koch realised that it was the microbe that caused the anthrax. But would it be possible to produce a vaccine?

Louis was sure that he and his assistants could make a vaccine. But it was not easy. They spent months trying to grow a form of the bacteria that was weak enough to use as a vaccine. At last, Louis found a method to create a safe culture. After tests in the laboratory, he was ready to show his new vaccine to the world.

Before the demonstration, Louis wrote to his son:

"*If there is a truly clear-cut success, it will be one of the most wonderful achievements of science and its application [use] in this century...*"

The world watched

On 5 May 1881, crowds gathered at a farm near the French town of Melun to see Louis demonstrate his possible cure for anthrax. Louis appeared confident but was probably nervous in front of the doubtful crowd. They watched him begin his experiment:

STAGE 1 (5–17 MAY): *25 of 50 sheep were given the vaccine.*

STAGE 2 (31 MAY): *all 50 sheep were injected with anthrax.*

This drawing shows Louis vaccinating sheep during his experiment in 1881.

Waiting for news

On 1 June a worried Louis paced up and down his laboratory in Paris waiting for the vaccine results. After a sleepless night, he received a note from the farm. It said that 18 of the non-vaccinated sheep had died, and all the vaccinated sheep were alive. "A tremendous success", it said. Sixty-year-old Louis was delighted, and relieved.

Wanted by the world

The vaccine worked with cows and oxen, too. Throughout the world, farmers asked for the vaccine for their animals. In 1882, 300,000 sheep and 80,000 oxen were vaccinated against anthrax in France alone.

A knock at the door

Louis had been studying rabies on and off for five years. He was keen to develop a cure for the disease that killed human beings. On 6 July 1885, a mother brought her young son to Louis' laboratory in Paris. The boy had been bitten by a dog with rabies. She begged Louis to help. Louis was worried. His rabies vaccine had only been tested on animals so far. But the boy's mother insisted he try it.

After being given the vaccine, the boy survived. The vaccine was to be Louis' last major discovery.

Louis and a group of English children he saved with his rabies vaccine.

Rabies

Rabies is caught with a bite from a rabies-infected animal, such as a dog. It affects the brain, and causes madness and other terrifying **symptoms**.

WHAT LOUIS LEFT BEHIND

Louis was recognized for his achievements in his final years. In 1884, the first biography of Louis was published. In 1888, a new research centre for Louis opened in Paris. It was named the Pasteur Institute. It was to become very important as a place where Louis' students and supporters could continue his work.

Last days

In 1894, at the age of 72, Louis was still working on **vaccines**. But in 1895, he had to retire after another **stroke**. Although unwell, he was able to enjoy time with his family before he died later that year.

By 1885, when this photograph was taken of him, Pasteur was well known and admired for his amazing discoveries.

Hard work

Louis' hard work, even through illness, was one reason for his great success. However, because work always came first, his family may have suffered. His wife, Marie, once wrote to her son: "Your father is as preoccupied as ever; he hardly speaks to me, sleeps little, and rises at dawn."

Great achievements

Today, we have much to thank Louis for. Without Louis' **pasteurization**, a glass of milk would not be as safe as it is today. His **proof** that **microbes** cause diseases has led to the cure of many illnesses. Because of Louis, cleanliness is now an important part of our everyday life. It has meant that diseases are far less likely to spread. Many more **vaccinations** now keep us safe from terrible diseases such as measles and **hepatitis B**.

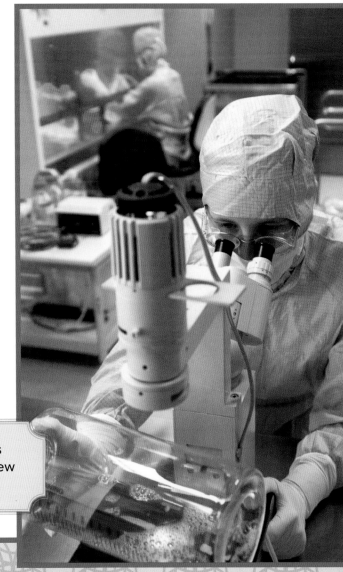

More than 100 years after Pasteur's death, scientists are still producing new vaccines for people and animals.

TIMELINES

Pasteur's life

1822 Louis Pasteur is born on 27 December, in Dole, France

1827 Pasteur moves with his family to the French town of Arbois

1838 Pasteur goes to school in Paris but returns to Arbois in 6 weeks because he is homesick

1842 Pasteur returns to school in Paris and passes his exams

1843–1846 Pasteur studies and teaches at the École Normale

1848 Jeanne Pasteur, Pasteur's mother, dies

1849 Pasteur moves to Strasbourg in January for a job as professor of **chemistry** at the university. In May he marries Marie Laurent

1850 Jeanne, the first of Pasteur's four daughters, is born

1851 Pasteur's only son, Jean-Baptiste, is born

1854 Pasteur begins researching fermentation of beet juice

1857 Pasteur is appointed director of scientific studies at the École Normale, Paris. He starts to study **fermentation** and spontaneous generation.

1859 Eldest daughter, Jeanne, dies of typhoid fever

1865 Pasteur's father and then youngest daughter, Camille, die

1866 Pasteur's third daughter, Cécile, dies

1868 Pasteur saves the silk-making industry in France after three summers of research

1880 Pasteur produces a **vaccine** for chicken **cholera**

1881 Pasteur successfully demonstrates his **anthrax** vaccine

1885 Pasteur injects a boy, Joseph Meister, with a rabies vaccine and saves his life

1888 Pasteur Institute opens in Paris. Pasteur is made director of the Institute.

1895 Pasteur has a **stroke** and dies 28 September, aged 72.

World timeline

1796 Edward Jenner gives the first **vaccination** (against smallpox)

1815 Napoleon's French army are defeated at the Battle of Waterloo

1830–1848 Louis-Philippe I is king of France

1831 Charles Darwin starts a voyage around the world

1833 Slavery is abolished (ended) in Britain

1848 The Californian Gold Rush happens. The **revolution** in Paris brings an end of the reign of King Louis-Philippe I

1852 Napoleon III becomes **emperor** of France. Livingstone discovers the Victoria Falls in Africa

1861–1865 The American Civil War happens

1863–1875 Cholera spreads through Europe and Africa

1865 Joseph Lister invents the first **antiseptic** (carbolic acid)

1870–1871 The **Franco-Prussian War** happens. Napoleon III's rule comes to an end.

1876 Robert Koch discovers the microbe that causes anthrax

1896 The first vaccine for typhoid fever is used

GLOSSARY

acid substance that has a sour or bitter taste. Stronger acids are poisonous and dangerous.

anthrax disease caused by a bacterium that can kill animals and people but mainly affects farm animals

antiseptic liquid or cream that kills or stops germs spreading. You put antiseptic cream on a cut or sore.

bacteria lots of microbes, some of which can cause diseases. One of these is called a bacterium.

cell small part of a living thing

chemist expert in chemistry or someone who makes and sells medicines. Today, shops that sell medicines are called chemists, or pharmacies.

chemistry study of substances and how they mix and react to each other. You can study chemistry at school.

cholera disease caused by bacteria that causes symptoms such as sickness and diarrhoea. Cholera easily spreads through dirty water.

chrysalis another name for a cocoon, which a caterpillar makes and wraps around itself

crystal solid structure with flat sides. Snow crystals are beautiful and have fancy shapes.

culture microbes grown in a laboratory. Louis used chicken broth to grow some of his cultures.

emperor ruler of a group of countries or people. Napoleon III was emperor of France from 1852–1870.

excrement animal or human waste matter passed out of the body

fermentation process in which sugars are broken down. Fermentation is used to make beer and wine.

fermented substance that has changed because the sugars in it have broken down. Fermented grapes are used to make wine.

filter like a sieve, a filter gets bits out of a liquid. Filters can also be used to get tiny bits out of the air.

Franco-Prussian war war between France and Prussia (Prussia was a German country in the past)

gas not a solid or a liquid. Air is a mix of different gases.

germs (also called microbes) tiny living creatures that cause diseases. Washing your hands gets rid of germs.

government group of people in charge of a country. The people in government are called politicians.

hepatitis B disease cause by a virus. Hepatitis B affects the liver.

hygiene keeping clean and healthy

infection caused by a microbe and can easily spread from person to person. Cholera is an infectious disease.

laboratory room used for scientific experiments

microbes another word for germs. Microbes are too small to see without a microscope.

microscope piece of equipment that makes tiny things look larger

paratartrate acid substance that is similar to tartrate acid. Louis found that paratartrate acid is made up of two types of crystal.

pasteurization way of killing microbes in a drink, without spoiling its taste. The milk we drink is pasteurized.

physics study of matter and energy. People who study physics are called physicists.

proof information that shows something is true or not true. Experiments are used to find proof.

rector Christian person who is in charge of a church. A rector organizes church services.

revolution time when people in a country fight to change the person or people in power. In France there have been two major revolutions: The French Revolution (1789–1799) and the Second French Revolution (1848).

riot disturbance caused by a large crowd of people

sterilize clean something to destroy microbes and prevent infection

stroke medical word for when a blood vessel to the brain bursts or gets blocked. Louis suffered from two strokes.

symptom sign of an illness. A high temperature is a symptom of many illnesses.

tanner someone who makes leather. A tanner's workshop is called a tannery.

tartrate acid substance found in plants and fruit, such as grapes. Tartrate acid is made up of crystals.

typhoid fever disease caused by bacteria, which gives the sufferer a very high temperature. Two of Louis' daughters died of typhoid fever.

vaccination way of giving a vaccine. Vaccinations are given to children to stop them getting serious diseases.

vaccine weaker form of a germ that is injected into a person's body to help fight a stronger form of the same germ

yeast fungi used in brewing and baking. Yeast is added to bread dough to make the bread rise.

WANT TO KNOW MORE?

Books

The Fight Against Microbes: Pasteur's Story, C. Birmingham
(Mathew Price Ltd, 2006)

Giants of Science: Joseph Lister, Peggy J. Parks (Blackbirch Press, 2005)

Has a Cow Saved Your Life?, Deborah Underwood (Raintree, 2006)

A Painful History of Medicine (series), John Townsend (Raintree, 2007)

Scientists Who Made History: Louis Pasteur, Liz Gogerly
(Raintree, 2002)

World's Worst Germs, Anna Claybourne (Raintree, 2005)

Websites

www.Pasteur.fr/english.html
The Pasteur Institute website has information about Louis, and work
done at the Institute by scientists since Louis' death.

www.invent.org
Search for other inventors at the Inventors' National Hall of Fame.

www.microbeworld.org
This site has lots of pictures and facts about microbes.

www.microscopy-uk.org.uk/intro/index.html
Learn all about the history of microscopes and how to use one.

Places to visit

The Museum of Applications of Pastorian Research
3, boulevard Raymond Poincaré and 3, avenue Pasteur
92430 Marnes-La-Coquette
France
A museum built around the room where Pasteur died.
It tells the story of the fight against infectious diseases,
through the work of Pasteur and his Institute.

The Pasteur Institute Museum
25, rue du Docteur Roux
75015 Paris
France
Go on a guided tour of Pasteur's home in Paris.

INDEX